WOMEN WHO WON'T BE SILENCED
THE STORIES OF STRONG WOMEN

MALALA YOUSAFZAI

LUCENT
PRESS

ELLEN CREAGER

Published in 2019 by
Lucent Press, an Imprint of Greenhaven Publishing, LLC
353 3rd Avenue
Suite 255
New York, NY 10010

Developed and produced for Rosen by BlueApple*Works* Inc.

Managing Editor for BlueApple*Works*: Melissa McClellan
Designer: Tibor Choleva
Photo Research: Jane Reid
Editor: Marcia Abramson

Photo Credits: cover, p. 4, 7 Southbank Centre/Creative Commons; title page DFID - UK Department for International Development/Creative Commons; background Vladitto/Shutterstock; p. 8 JStone/Shutterstock.com; p. 10, 12–13 Shahid Khan/Shutterstock; p. 11 DoD photo by: SRA BETHANN HUNT, USAF/Public Domain; p. 14 SRA Gerald B. Johnson, United States Department of Defense/Public Domain; p.16, 23 Edwin Koo/Keystone Press; p. 18–19, 19 inset Asianet-Pakistan/Shutterstock.com; p. 20 Sgt. Joseph J. Johnson (U.S. armed forces)/Public Domain; p. 24 Claude Truong-Ngoc/Wikimedia Commons - cc-by-sa-3.0; p. 27 Tony Hisgett/Creative Commons; p. 28–29 Peter J. Souza/Executive Office of the President of the United States/Public Domain; p. 30 Dennis Van Tine/Keystone Press; p. 31 Fox Searchlight Pictures/Photofest; p. 33 UK Foreign and Commonwealth Office/Open Government Licence v1.0; p. 34, 48, 50, 52 DFID - UK Department for International Development/Creative Commons; p. 36 Claude Truong-Ngoc/Wikimedia Commons - cc-by-sa-3.0; p. 38 Poppe, Cornelius/Keystone Press; p. 40 Bair175/Creative Commons; p. 42 David Kawai/Keystone Press; p. 44 Irfan/Keystone Press; p. 45/Creative Commons; p. 46–47 Glen Stubbe/Keystone Press; p. 49 Capt. John Severns, U.S. Air Force/Public Domain; p. 53 Karl_Sonnenberg/Shutterstock.com; p. 55 JStone/Shutterstock.com; p. 56 Dave Warren/Keystone Press

Cataloging-in-Publication-Data
Names: Creager, Ellen.
Title: Malala Yousafzai / Ellen Creager.
Description: New York : Lucent Press, 2019. | Series: Women who won't be silenced: the stories of strong women | Includes glossary and index.
Identifiers: ISBN 9781534566477 (pbk.) | ISBN 9781534566484 (library bound) | ISBN 9781534566491 (ebook)
Subjects: LCSH: Yousafzai, Malala, 1997---Juvenile literature. | Young women--Education--Pakistan--Biography--Juvenile literature. | Women social reformers--Pakistan--Biography--Juvenile literature.
Classification: LCC HQ1745.5.Z75 C743 2019 | DDC 371.822095491 B--dc23

Manufactured in the United States of America

CPSIA Compliance Information: Batch #BW19KL: For Further Information contact: Greenhaven Publishing LLC, New York, New York at 1-844-317-7404.

CONTENTS

CHAPTER 1

WHO IS MALALA YOUSAFZAI?

With eloquence and courage far beyond her years, Malala Yousafzai has dedicated her life to helping girls go to school. Her magnetic personality has made her one of the most famous people in the world.

Now in her early 20s, she became widely known at age 11 for speaking up for girls' education in her homeland of Pakistan. She spoke so strongly and so convincingly that her life soon was threatened.

In 2012, she was shot in the head by a member of the Taliban, a militant **Islamic** group. That group believed that girls should never go to school. Malala almost died from her wound.

Rushed to England by plane, the 15-year-old's life was saved by skilled doctors. Since then, she has recovered and gone on to speak even more forcefully for her cause.

The shooting may have silenced another person, but for Malala, the opposite was true. She felt as though her survival was a gift that she must use.

"I believe in the power of raising your voice," she has said many times.

In 2014, at just 17 years old, she won the Nobel Peace Prize. She was the youngest person ever to win any Nobel Prize.

Today, through her nonprofit Malala Fund, she advocates for girls' education around the world. She also is a student at the University of Oxford in England, studying philosophy, politics, and economics.

In 2018, she was thrilled to return to her beloved Pakistan for a visit. After a five-year absence, she even saw her old house in her hometown of Mingora.

Malala believes that when girls are educated they gain freedom and strength. Girls may be young, but they are not powerless, she repeats again and again.

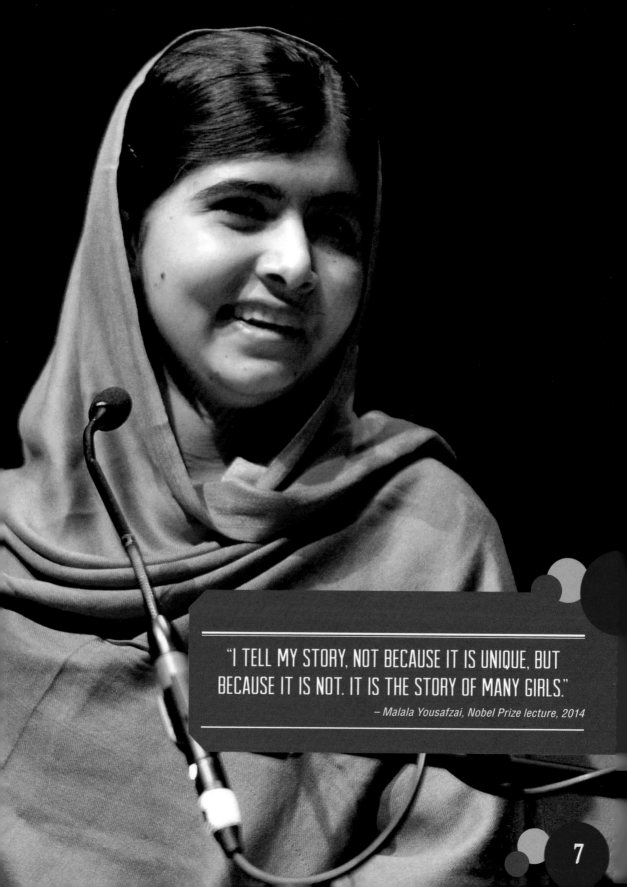

"I TELL MY STORY, NOT BECAUSE IT IS UNIQUE, BUT BECAUSE IT IS NOT. IT IS THE STORY OF MANY GIRLS."

– Malala Yousafzai, Nobel Prize lecture, 2014

Malala has been inspired by her father Ziauddin, who was campaigning for girls' education long before he had children of his own. He began sharing his life lessons with her when she was just a little girl.

CHAPTER 2

GROWING UP IN PAKISTAN

The birth of a baby girl is not always a happy event in Pakistan, where boys are prized. Yet for this baby girl born at home in July of 1997, parents Ziauddin and Toor Pekai Yousafzai could not have been prouder.

Her father named her Malala, after a famous female war hero, Malalai of Maiwand. Some relatives did not like the name because it means "grief-stricken." But Malala's father had a feeling she would be special. And he treated her that way.

Malala grew up toddling around the schoolroom. Her father owned a private school, and for a time, the family lived upstairs. The parents had little money, but they had a lot of big plans. Soon, Malala had two brothers, Khushal and Atal. Her early childhood was full of games and fun, with lots of family and friends nearby or visiting their home in Mingora in the scenic Swat Valley.

> "I CHOSE THIS LIFE. IT WAS NOT FORCED ON ME."
>
> — *Malala Yousafzai, interview in the documentary* He Named Me Malala, *2015*

The Swat River runs through Malala's picturesque hometown of Mingora, which has about 331,000 residents.

When Malala watched TV, her favorite show was *Shaka Laka Boom Boom* about a boy with a magic pencil who could make his wishes come true. Yet soon, distant world events and ugly local problems shook the valley. When Malala was just 5 years old, a local **mullah** complained that girls should not go to school because it was against Islam. Although nearly everyone in Pakistan, including Malala's family, was Muslim, **zealots** said they were not religious enough. By the time Malala was 7, boys and girls could no longer be educated together.

THE PASHTUN CONNECTION

Malala's last name, Yousafzai, is also a tribal name for her Pashtun people in Pakistan. The Pashtuns are an ancient group that pre-dates the founding of Pakistan itself, dating back thousands of years. Pashtuns are Muslims. They are known for their hospitality and family loyalty. They also are known for their "nang," or honor – a fierce pride and a vow never to forgive or forget a wrong.

The extremist group the Taliban was created by Pashtuns. But Malala also is Pashtun. She has said she forgives the man who shot her, saying "the best revenge is forgiveness."

Today, many Pashtuns are tired of revenge, wars, and conflict.

About 14 million Pashtuns live in Afghanistan and 31 million in Pakistan, in a wide area sometimes called Pashtunistan.

LIVING AMID DRAMA AND BEAUTY

Malala grew up in a region of northwest Pakistan called the Swat Valley. It was known as the "Switzerland of the East" for its green, mountainous beauty and lovely four-season weather. Before conflict came, the Swat Valley was a pretty place to live and popular with Pakistani and foreign tourists. It even had a ski resort.

The Swat Valley is in Pakistan's northern province of Khyber Pakhtunkhwa. It is less than 100 miles (161 km) from the border with neighboring Afghanistan. It also is not far from the famous Khyber Pass, a rugged road used by centuries of traders and invaders.

Perhaps the most famous town in the region is Abbottabad. One night in 2011, U.S. Navy Seals attacked a house there and killed Osama bin Laden, mastermind of the 9/11 attacks. He had been safely living there for up to six years, hiding from the world, just 60 miles (97 km) from Malala's home.

People have lived in the lush Swat Valley for more than 2,000 years.

Benazir Bhutto, the first female prime minister of Pakistan, has inspired Malala since she was in fourth grade. Malala wore one of Bhutto's shawls for her 2013 speech at the United Nations. Unlike Malala, Bhutto did not survive an assassination attempt. She died in 2007.

TALIBAN TROUBLE

After a big earthquake shook Pakistan in 2005, some said that God was angry and people needed to be even more religious. By 2007, when Malala was 10, the extremist group the Taliban arrived and took over her city. They preached that books, TVs, and DVDs should be burned. They said there should be no shaving for men, no vaccinations, no board games, and no shopping. They said all females should cover their faces, women should stay home, and girls should not go to school. They publicly whipped those who did not obey.

They told Malala's father to close his Khushal Public School.

At first, Malala's father and many other citizens spoke up and kept the schools going. Malala was an especially excellent student. People noticed the little girl with the big smile and musical laughter.

Public speaking competitions were popular in the schools, and Malala had already started giving speeches. Her father wrote her very first speech. After that, she found her own voice.

"I started writing my own speeches and changing the way I deliver them, from my heart rather than from a sheet of paper," she later wrote in her autobiography.

"LET US PICK UP OUR BOOKS AND OUR PENS. THEY ARE OUR MOST POWERFUL WEAPONS."

– Malala Yousafzai, speech to United Nations, 2013

As life got bleaker, she studied even harder in school: "It was school that kept me going in those dark days."

In 2008, the Taliban began blowing up girls' schools. They killed people. They threw acid in people's faces. They hounded girls to stay home. Most girls dropped out. By the end of 2008, the Taliban had blown up 400 schools in Pakistan.

Malala's happy childhood had taken a dark turn.

The Taliban ordered all women and girls over age 7 to wear a burqa, a head-to-toe covering, in public. For some, the burqa became a symbol of Taliban rule and the way women were treated.

CHAPTER 3

FIGHTING FOR CHANGE

When the Taliban began terrorizing her part of Pakistan, Malala was just 10 years old. Her father joined city leaders to keep schools open and the city functioning. He even gave international radio interviews to the British Broadcasting Corporation (BBC) and Voice of America. Then Malala herself began to give interviews on Pakistani television about trying to go to school despite fear of the Taliban.

She was determined. "If I am speaking for my rights, for the rights of girls, I am not doing anything wrong. It is my duty to do so," she later recalled.

> "I HAVE THE RIGHT OF EDUCATION. I HAVE THE RIGHT TO SING. I HAVE THE RIGHT TO TALK. I HAVE THE RIGHT TO GO TO MARKET. I HAVE THE RIGHT TO SPEAK UP."
>
> – Malala Yousafzai, interview with CNN, 2011

WHO ARE THE TALIBAN?

The Taliban are an extremist **Sunni** Muslim group in the countries of Pakistan and Afghanistan. Founded in 1994 by hard-liners who thought their fellow Muslims were not **devout** enough, the Taliban controlled Afghanistan from the mid-1990s until 2001.

They also took over Malala's town in the Swat Valley of Pakistan from 2007 to 2009. They imposed harsh restrictions on the people, including closing girls' schools.

The man who shot Malala in 2012 was a member of the Taliban.

Today, the Taliban still cause trouble and terror in Pakistan and Afghanistan, where they maintain influence. The Taliban still oppose education for girls. They think that when girls learn, they think for themselves too much.

"THE WORLD NEEDS LEADERSHIP BASED ON SERVING HUMANITY —
NOT BASED ON HOW MANY WEAPONS YOU HAVE."

– Malala Yousafzai, speech to Canadian Parliament, 2017

Girls' schools were not the only targets of the Taliban. In December 2014, militants attacked Army Public School in Peshawar, Pakistan. Among the 145 who died, 132 were children. More than 100 others were injured and flooded local hospitals (inset). The school serves military families, and the Taliban bragged that they had killed many sons of military leaders who opposed them.

Some boys' schools delayed classes in February 2009 to show support for girls' education. The Taliban eased some restrictions on girls in primary school, but soon war broke out and people fled the Swat Valley. The government was able to reopen schools for boys and girls in August 2009.

In September that year, she gave a talk at a press club in nearby Peshawar. Her speech was called "How Dare the Taliban Take Away My Basic Right to Education?" It riveted the nation.

Soon, the Taliban threatened all girls' schools, saying they must close by January 15, 2009. Fifty thousand girls would not be able to go to school. Malala kept speaking out.

"The Taliban could take our pens and books, but they couldn't stop our minds from thinking," she later wrote.

A SECRET DIARY

As the Taliban cracked down, the BBC was looking for a girl to write a blog about what it was like to go to school under the extremists. Malala volunteered. The blog was written under an alias, Gul Makai, because it was too dangerous to use her real name. She also did not dare upload her diary directly. Instead, a BBC reporter would call her on a cell phone at night, she would talk to him, and he would write it up and post it on a site once a week called BBC **Urdu**.

He told her about Anne Frank's diary in World War II, and she was inspired. Her first post, on January 3, 2009, was titled, "I AM AFRAID."

She did not know it, but people all over the world began reading the blog, which was translated into English. She would write 35 entries between January and March.

By January 9, fewer than a dozen girls were left in Malala's class. On January 14, her school closed.

Malala participated in making two documentaries for the *New York Times* about her last day of school, this time using her real name.

"ONE CHILD, ONE TEACHER, ONE BOOK, ONE PEN CAN CHANGE THE WORLD."
– From Malala Yousafzai's book I Am Malala, *2013*

FLEEING DANGER

When the Taliban closed girls' schools, Pakistan was criticized around the world. To persuade the extremists to reopen at least the elementary girls' schools, government leaders agreed that the Taliban could impose harsh Islamic law in the Swat Valley. Soon, the Taliban was beating and killing people for doing anything they opposed. Then, Pakistan sent troops to the region. Fierce battles broke out. Things got so dangerous that Malala's family and 2 million others had to flee in May, seeking shelter with relatives and friends in other towns.

They went home in August 2009 when the government promised it had gotten rid of the Taliban. Many buildings were destroyed, but Malala's school was still standing. She went back to school. Word got out that Malala had written the famous BBC blog.

Life settled down, but the Taliban and their harsh influence still simmered underneath the surface of society.

"ISLAM SAYS EVERY GIRL AND EVERY BOY SHOULD GO TO SCHOOL. IN THE QURAN IT IS WRITTEN, GOD WANTS US TO HAVE KNOWLEDGE. HE WANTS US TO KNOW WHY THE SKY IS BLUE AND ABOUT OCEANS AND STARS."

– From Malala Yousafzai's book I Am Malala, 2013

Malala's family had to split up, but at least they had places to stay. Many of the 2.4 milllion refugees from the Swat Valley ended up in crowded camps like this one in Swabi, Pakistan, in May 2009.

DEATH THREATS

In 2011, Malala won Pakistan's first ever National Peace Prize. Her father was proud. But her mother feared the attention, worried that Malala would become a target. Soon, a journalist told Malala's father that the Taliban indeed was threatening to kill her. Police even collected a file of death threats against her.

The family thought of sending her away to boarding school, but Malala did not want to go. She became cautious. She had bad dreams. She prayed a lot. But she kept speaking out and going to her local school as usual. At 15, she had a lot of exams coming up.

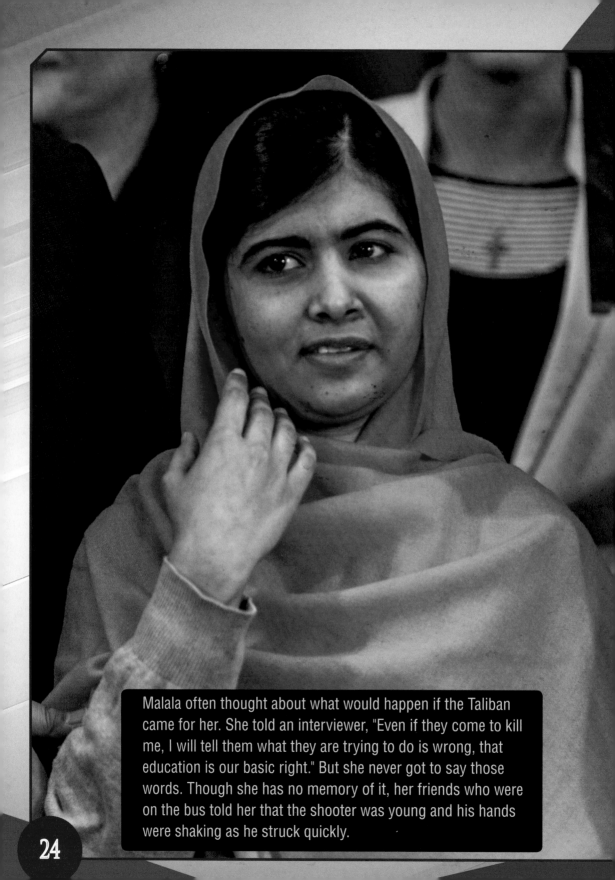

Malala often thought about what would happen if the Taliban came for her. She told an interviewer, "Even if they come to kill me, I will tell them what they are trying to do is wrong, that education is our basic right." But she never got to say those words. Though she has no memory of it, her friends who were on the bus told her that the shooter was young and his hands were shaking as he struck quickly.

CHAPTER 4

SHOT BY THE TALIBAN

On October 9, 2012, it was exam day at school. Malala, 15, took one of her tests and then boarded the school bus, sitting with her friends near the back. Her little brother Atal wanted to ride with them, but there was no room, so he had to walk home.

The bus pulled away. The girls chattered. Then, two men stepped into the road in front of the bus.

"Who is Malala?" one of them asked.

Nobody spoke, but some girls' eyes drifted her way.

The man shot her in the head. Bullets also hit another girl's palm and grazed a third girl's arm.

Badly bleeding, Malala slumped over. The bus driver sped to the local hospital. Everyone was crying and screaming.

"I HAVE BEEN GIVEN A NEW LIFE, AND THIS LIFE IS A SACRED LIFE."
– Malala Yousafzai, speech to the United Nations

CLOSE TO DEATH

At the hospital, doctors first were relieved because the bullet had not gone directly into Malala's brain. It had entered her head near her eye, then back out into her shoulder. Still, they quickly flew her by helicopter to a military hospital in nearby Peshawar. There, neurosurgeon Colonel Junaid Khan realized that Malala's brain was swelling. Pieces of bone were piercing her brain. He had to operate to save her life, removing part of her skull.

She survived the surgery. But soon, her body began to fail. More doctors came, including two British doctors who happened to be visiting Pakistan, Dr. Javid Kayani and Dr. Fiona Reynolds. In an induced **coma** and battling infection, Malala was airlifted again to another Pakistani hospital under tight security. There, Dr. Reynolds and Dr. Kayani tried to stabilize her.

All the while, the Taliban threatened that anyone who helped her or the government would be killed.

Worried she might die, the Pakistani Army decided to send her to a British hospital. The country of the United Arab Emirates offered its royal plane to transport her. On October 15, an unconscious Malala was flown thousands of

Queen Elizabeth Hospital in Birmingham often treats soldiers injured in combat. Malala's injury was similar, so doctors there knew what to do. The hospital is named not for Queen Elizabeth II but for her mother, who was also an Elizabeth.

miles to Queen Elizabeth Hospital in Birmingham, England. There, doctors watched, waited, and hoped.

Her worried family stayed behind in Pakistan, waiting for authorities to let them fly to their daughter's side.

10 THINGS THAT MIGHT SURPRISE YOU ABOUT MALALA

1. She is only five feet tall so she usually wears high heels.

2. She always wears a head scarf but never covers her face.

3. Her favorite color is pink.

4. As of 2018, she had 1.38 million Twitter followers.

5. She has a **cochlear implant** so her left ear, damaged in the shooting, can hear.

6. Her favorite book is *The Alchemist* by Paulo Coelho.

7. In 2015, the space agency NASA named an **asteroid** in her honor.

8. She knows card tricks.

9. Her native language is **Pashto**, but she also is fluent in Urdu and English.

10. She finally took driving lessons at age 20, in England.

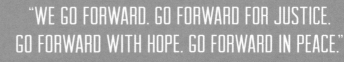
In 2013, Malala met with President Barack Obama, his wife, Michelle, and 15-year-old daughter Malia at the White House. Typical of Malala, she spoke not only of education but told the president that drone strikes were making terrorism worse in Pakistan.

A DAY NAMED AFTER MALALA

The United Nations has proclaimed July 12, Malala Yousafzai's birthday, as Malala Day. It was the same day she addressed the body in 2013. Every year on Malala Day, people around the world speak and act on behalf of girls' education.

July 12, 2013, was not only Malala Day at the United Nations but also a Youth Takeover. About 200 young advocates for education joined Malala for a day of activities at the UN. Similar events were held worldwide.

Malala is close to both parents, though her mother has been much less in the public eye. Toor Pekai says she feels that her daughter was reborn into a new life after the attack. Now Toor Pekai has a new life, too, She is studying English and wants to help others get an education, just like her daughter and husband.

A SECOND LIFE

The day after she arrived in England, Malala slowly regained consciousness. She could not talk at first. She did not know where she was. She was afraid her family was dead. She worried about how to pay for the hospital. Finally, doctors gave her a phone and she listened to her parents' voices back in Pakistan. They all cried. After 10 days, they finally joined her.

Her recovery was slow, but it amazed doctors.

During the next three months, Malala had more surgeries: one to put a new titanium plate in her skull, one to put an implant in her left ear so she could hear on that side again, and one to repair a torn facial nerve that had prevented her from smiling.

At first, her family was terrified that the bullet had caused brain damage and she would never be the same again. Her father blamed himself for putting Malala in harm's way.

Yet, she surprised everyone. Soon they saw that her brain was as powerful as ever. Her speech and sense of humor returned. Her smile returned. Her face would never be completely **symmetrical** again, but she was alive.

And she was even more determined to fight for the education of girls.

"I REASSURED MY MOTHER THAT IT DIDN'T MATTER TO ME IF MY FACE WAS NOT SYMMETRICAL. ME, WHO HAD ALWAYS CARED ABOUT MY APPEARANCE, HOW MY HAIR LOOKED. BUT WHEN YOU SEE DEATH, THINGS CHANGE. IT DOESN'T MATTER IF I CAN'T SMILE OR BLINK PROPERLY, I TOLD HER, I'M STILL ME, MALALA. THE IMPORTANT THING IS, GOD HAS GIVEN ME MY LIFE."

– From Malala Yousafzai's book I Am Malala, *2013*

Top officials from three countries – Britain, Pakistan, and the United Arab Emirates – visited Queen Elizabeth Hospital on October 29. Malala was not well enough to see them, but they spoke with her father and thanked the hospital's medical director.

GAINING STRENGTH

In early 2013, Malala was released from the hospital. Her family was offered a place to live in Birmingham, England, since it still was too dangerous to return to Pakistan. The government of Pakistan offered to pay all of Malala's medical bills.

Later that spring, Malala was well enough to enter Edgbaston High School for Girls in Birmingham. She kept speaking out on behalf of girls' education through her new nonprofit, Malala Fund.

"IN TERMS OF ACHIEVEMENTS, GETTING MY (UK HIGH SCHOOL EXAM) RESULTS AND LISTENING TO MY TEACHERS SAYING 'A'S AND A STARS' — IT WAS THE MOST BEAUTIFUL AND THE HAPPIEST MOMENT."

– *Malala Yousafzai, interview with* USA Today, *September 2015*

"I know God stopped me from going to the grave," she later wrote. "It feels like this life is a second life."

The teen girl that the Taliban had tried to murder for going to school had not only survived, but thrived. Their plan had backfired.

Instead of getting rid of Malala, the Taliban made her world famous.

Amazingly, just three years after being shot in the head, Malala would achieve all A's and A stars (same as A-plus) on high school exams in 10 subjects: biology, chemistry, physics, religious studies, history, geography, English language, English literature. and two math exams. She would go on to get A's on three more tough exams to gain entrance to a university.

> "WHEN THE WHOLE WORLD IS SILENT, EVEN ONE VOICE BECOMES POWERFUL."
>
> *– Malala Yousafzai, speech at Harvard, 2013*

Malala received the Sakharov Prize for Freedom of Thought from the European Parliament in 2013. (Look close and you'll see her at the podium in the center.) She was honored on November 20, World Children's Day. The prize is named for Andrei Sakharov, a scientist who stood up to the former Soviet Union.

Malala did not know it, but on the day the Taliban shot her, the world shifted. The Taliban bragged about the shooting and took credit for it. Some **conspiracy theorists** in the Muslim world said the shooting was faked or that she worked for the CIA.

The rest of the world was horrified.

Politicians like U.S. President Barack Obama and the Secretary General of the United Nations called the shootings reprehensible and disgusting. Celebrities like Angelina Jolie and Beyoncé sent good wishes. Thousands of regular people around the world sent cards, letters, packages, and even offers of adoption, not knowing that Malala already had parents!

Meanwhile, hundreds of journalists crowded outside her hospital, waiting for the latest word on her condition. News helicopters hovered overhead.

The world came together in its prayers.

After Malala recovered, she got so many awards and honors for humanitarian work and bravery she could barely remember them all. They came from foreign governments, from child advocates, and from universities.

One important award she got was the 2014 **Anne Frank** Award for Moral Courage.

Comparing Malala's bravery with Anne's courage during World War II, essayist Platon Poulas wrote, "In times of deep darkness, these two figures, these two teenage girls have risen, through their writing, as metaphorical moral compasses for thousands of people."

Malala received a plaque and a medal when she won the 2014 Nobel Peace Prize. The awards were created by scientist Alfred Nobel, the inventor of dynamite. He wanted his fortune to be used to benefit humanity after his death, so winners also receive a large cash prize.

CHAPTER 5

THE YOUNGEST NOBEL LAUREATE

On her 16th birthday, Malala spoke in front of a hushed crowd at the United Nations in New York. It was July 12, 2013. Her eloquence and grace stunned those who had not seen her speak before.

Wearing a pink **shalwar kameez** dress and shawl, she riveted the crowd with her **oratory**.

"The terrorists thought they would change my aims and stop my ambitions, but nothing changed in my life except this: weakness, fear, and hopelessness died. Strength, power, and courage was born," she said, her voice ringing out.

> "I AM PRETTY CERTAIN THAT I AM ALSO THE FIRST RECIPIENT OF THE NOBEL PEACE PRIZE WHO STILL FIGHTS WITH HER YOUNGER BROTHERS. I WANT THERE TO BE PEACE EVERYWHERE, BUT MY BROTHERS AND I ARE STILL WORKING ON THAT."
>
> – Malala Yousafzai, Nobel Prize lecture, 2014

Malala and Kailash Satyarthi (second from left) received Nobel prizes on December 19, 2014, in Norway.

"I am not against anyone, neither am I here to speak in terms of personal revenge against the Taliban or any other terrorist group. I'm here to speak up for the right of education for every child."

That year, she was named one of *Time* magazine's 100 most influential people in the world. She received awards from countless organizations.

She was nominated for the Nobel Peace Prize in 2013 and again in 2014, when she was 17.

One day, she was in chemistry class when she was called to the school office. She thought she was in trouble. Instead, they told her she had won the 2014 Nobel Peace Prize along with children's activist Kailash Satyarthi of India.

> "LET US BE THE FIRST GENERATION THAT DECIDES TO BE THE LAST THAT SEES EMPTY CLASSROOMS, LOST CHILDHOODS AND WASTED POTENTIALS."
>
> – *Malala Yousafzai, Nobel Prize lecture, 2014*

She was the first Pakistani, first Pashtun, and the youngest Nobel Prize winner ever. She finished the school day, then went home to a throng of reporters at her doorstep.

5 THINGS MALALA LIKES

In 2018, Malala answered questions on a webchat with Canadian students. She revealed:

1. Her favorite athlete is Swiss tennis player Roger Federer
2. Her current favorite TV show is *The Big Bang Theory*
3. Her favorite food is her mother's rice and chicken curry
4. Her favorite class at University of Oxford is philosophy
5. Her favorite cricket team is the Pakistan national team (especially its former captain Shahid Afridi)

Malala became an honorary citizen of Canada in April 2017. "Malala, your story is an inspiration to us all," said Justin Trudeau, Canada's prime minister (right). She was only the sixth person, as well as the youngest, to receive honorary Canadian citizenship.

"I USED TO THINK I HAD TO WAIT TO BE AN ADULT TO LEAD. BUT I'VE LEARNED THAT EVEN A CHILD'S VOICE CAN BE HEARD AROUND THE WORLD."

– Malala Yousafzai, speech to Canadian Parliament, 2017

When she later accepted the prize in Norway, her words implored the world to act: "This award is not just for me," she said. "It is for those forgotten children who want education. It is for those frightened children who want peace. It is for those voiceless children who want change.

"I am here to stand up for their rights, to raise their voice… it is not time to pity them. It is not time to pity them. It is time to take action so it becomes the last time, the last time, so it becomes the last time that we see a child deprived of education."

As Malala was being named the winner of the Nobel Peace Prize in October 2014, girls were able to study in government-run schools like this one in southwest Pakistan.

A NOBEL RECORD

The Nobel Prizes are awarded each year to people who have done the most to "benefit mankind" in the fields of medicine, literature, physics, chemistry, and peace.

The average age of a winner is 59.

When Malala Yousafzai won the 2014 Nobel Peace Prize at age 17, she became the youngest person ever to win any Nobel Prize. She replaced Lawrence Bragg as the youngest winner (he won the 1915 Nobel Prize for Physics at age 25).

Other young winners have included Martin Luther King Jr. (1964 Nobel Peace Prize at age 35) and scientist Marie Curie (1903 Nobel Prize in Physics at age 36).

Visitors to the Nobel Institute in Oslo, Norway, can see a gallery of Nobel Peace Prize winners, who are called Nobel **laureates**. The institute has a large library of peace-related materials and hosts events to bring people together.

"I STAND WITH GIRLS, AS SOMEONE WHO KNOWS WHAT IT'S LIKE TO FLEE YOUR HOME AND WONDER IF YOU'LL EVER GO BACK TO SCHOOL."

– *Malala Yousafzai, speech to Canadian Parliament, 2017*

THE MALALA FUND

In October 2013, Malala, her father, and family friend Shiza Shahid started the Malala Fund. Its aim is simple: 12 years of quality education for every girl in the world. The fund is run by a board of directors. Malala is the public face of the fund. Its focus is on programs that benefit girls' secondary education, especially in Pakistan, Afghanistan, India, Nigeria, and countries hosting Syrian refugees.

Between 2014 and 2018, Malala met with girls in Nigeria and Rwanda, opened a school in a Syrian refugee camp in Lebanon, and promoted girls' education on a "Girl Power Trip" for five months in 2017. In 2018, she opened a girls' school in Shangla, Pakistan.

Malala donated her approximately $700,000 Nobel Prize winnings to the Malala Fund. The fund also has benefited from big donations and partnerships from many companies, governments, and individual donors.

Malala surprised girls who were learning about her when she visited the Newcomer Academy in Minneapolis, Minnesota, in July 2016. Most of the students were refugees from Somalia. "They inspired me because they have courage. Some have been to more than six countries. It's a really hard time in your life when you don't know who will welcome you, who will accept you," Malala said.

BOOKS NOT BULLETS MOVEMENT

On her 18th birthday, Malala Yousafzai asked girls to upload a photo of themselves with their favorite books to Twitter, using the hashtag #booksnotbullets.

Why? She wanted to make the point that if every government in the world stopped military spending for just 8 days, it would raise $39 billion that could give 12 years of free education to every child in the world.

Malala and Indian actress Freida Pinto (second from left) joined a panel discussion on girls' rights at a new event called the Girl Summit in London in July 2014. Like Malala, Pinto campaigns to protect the rights of women and girls.

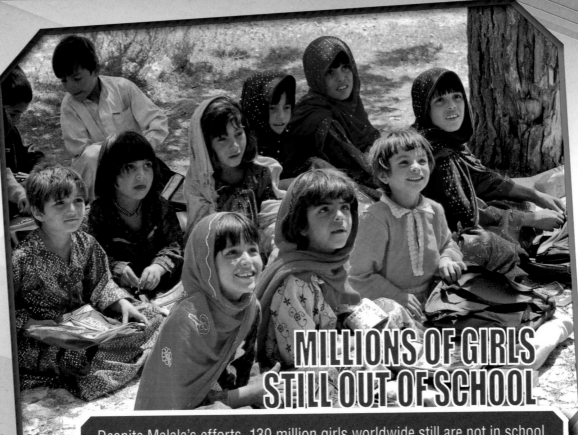

MILLIONS OF GIRLS STILL OUT OF SCHOOL

Despite Malala's efforts, 130 million girls worldwide still are not in school. Either they never started, or they dropped out because of war, lack of school buildings, or family pressure.

Statistics are particularly dire in Pakistan, Malala's native country. In 2018, more than half of girls over age 15 could not read. More than 13 million girls were out of school. In rural areas, only 1 in 4 girls go to school, according to the U.S. Council on Foreign Relations.

The worst countries for children being out of school are Nigeria, Pakistan, India, the Sudan, Ethiopia, and Indonesia, a 2016 United Nations report found.

Meanwhile, nearly as many boys are not in school – mostly because they have dropped out by high school or because war pulls them away from their studies.

Malala says she plans to continue her mission after college — and that might include becoming prime minister of Pakistan someday.

THE FUTURE

In 2015, a documentary about Malala Yousafzai's life, *He Named Me Malala,* was released in 175 countries, translated into 11 languages. Since then, her profile has grown even larger – and her life has become more complex.

She continues to give speeches and do interviews (she reportedly charges $165,000 per speech). She continues to raise money for the Malala Fund. In 2017 she also released a children's book, *Malala's Magic Pencil.*

But her biggest changes have been in her personal life.

"WHY DO LEADERS ACCEPT THAT FOR CHILDREN IN DEVELOPING COUNTRIES, ONLY BASIC LITERACY IS SUFFICIENT, WHEN THEIR OWN CHILDREN DO HOMEWORK IN ALGEBRA, MATHEMATICS, SCIENCE AND PHYSICS?"

– *Malala Yousafzai, Nobel lecture, 2014*

Malala visited the UK Department for International Development in January 2016 to talk about girls' education and the need to involve local people. In 2017, she launched a worldwide campaign to do exactly that.

In 2017, she entered the University of Oxford in England, studying politics, philosophy and economics. At age 20, she finally moved away from her family for the first time. She lived in a dormitory, doing regular college-student things like joining the cricket club and listening to music.

In the spring of 2018, her family flew back to Pakistan for the first time in more than five years for a visit. Under high security, the family saw the capital, Islamabad, and their former home in the Swat Valley.

I AM MALALA BOOK

In the fall of 2013, Malala Yousafzai released an autobiography, *I Am Malala: The Girl Who Stood Up for Education and Was Shot by the Taliban*. Co-written with British journalist Christina Lamb, the bestselling book recounted Malala's life up to the time she was shot and the months afterward.

The book came out a year before she won the Nobel Peace Prize.

It sold more than 1.8 million copies.

In 2016, an updated version of the book came out for young readers, with a new co-writer, Patricia McCormick. It had a gentler title: *I Am Malala: How One Girl Stood Up for Education and Changed the World*.

If one man can destroy everything, why can't one girl change it? -Malala Yousafzai #womensmarchla

Malala can't be everywhere, but her words are. For example, a protester at the 2017 Women's March in Los Angeles carried a sign (right) that quoted Malala.

SPEECH TO THE NATION

In Pakistan, Malala gave a televised speech to the nation. In a mixture of English, Pashto, and Urdu languages she expressed how thrilled she was to be back. Then Malala did something she never does during speeches – she broke down in tears.

She could not stop her heartfelt feelings from showing.

Most people in Pakistan supported Malala's visit, but some expressed hate. **Social media trolls** claimed her injuries had been faked or she was a Western pawn. Other Pakistanis were simply tired of hearing about Malala. In any case, Pakistan still was not safe enough for the family to return permanently.

As for the fate of the man who shot Malala, he and other plotters were believed to be hiding in Afghanistan. Only two men were convicted of being involved, and neither was the gunman.

"GOING BACK TO PAKISTAN AFTER 5 1/2 YEARS WAS THE MOST BEAUTIFUL AND EXCITING TIME FOR ME AND MY FAMILY. I THINK JUST GOING THERE AND GOING TO MY HOME AND SEEING THE STREET, MY ROOM, MY OLD TROPHIES, DINING PLACE, EVERYTHING AGAIN WAS THE MOST BEAUTIFUL MOMENT OF MY LIFE."

– Malala Yousafzai, interview with Globe and Mail, *Toronto, 2018*

MOVING ON

In 2018, Malala completed another book about girls, *We Are Displaced: True Stories of Refugee Lives*.

She continued to raise money for the Malala Fund and travel the world visiting girls' schools. She even agreed to be godmother to a new cruise ship in exchange for support for the fund from the Celebrity Cruises company.

Now older and more media savvy, she did many interviews on U.S. and Canadian television, mixing her talk about girls' education with demonstrations of her card trick ability and wry sense of humor. One thing Malala never talked about? Boys or boyfriends.

Despite that, she was growing up.

Today, Malala is no longer a brave and astonishing little girl. She is a brave and astonishing woman.

Her future likely will hold more surprises.

Malala's mission includes encouraging others to tell their stories and become activists. Ahmad Nahwaz (left), a survivor of the Army Public School attack, is one of them. She has inspired him to "be the voice of all the children," Ahmad says. Malala and her family hosted a reception in Birmingham on the anniversary of the Peshawar attack in 2015. Muhammad Ibrahim (seated), another survivor, was also a guest. Supporters wore white poppies, which are often used as an international symbol of peace.

MALALA'S FATHER

The most important person in Malala's life is her father, Ziauddin Yousafzai. He travels with her nearly everywhere. He is her biggest cheerleader, support system, and believer. He was the first person she asked about when she woke from her coma after being shot.

Malala credits her father with giving her the freedom to be herself, even as a little girl. She quotes her father often: "Don't ask me what I did for my daughter, ask me what I did not do. I did not clip her wings."

Ziauddin Yousafzai owned several private schools in their town of Mingora. He was born (like Malala's mother Toor Pekai), in a small village in northwest Pakistan's Swat Valley. Although Malala's mother could not read or write, Ziauddin Yousafzai went to college. Like Malala, he is a skilled public speaker and educational activist.

Today, he lives with his wife and two sons, Khushal and Atal, in Birmingham, England. Yet, he still is not far from Malala, who lives and studies at the University of Oxford.

"WE ARE REALLY TIRED OF THESE WARS."
— *Malala Yousafzai, speech at United Nations, 2013*

RECOGNITION

Malala Yousafzai is barely in her 20s, yet she has received many awards for her bravery and work. Among them:

2011:

National Youth Peace Prize, Pakistan

2012:

Sitara-e-Shujaat award for civilian bravery, from the government of Pakistan

Mother Teresa Memorial Award for Social Justice

Rome Prize for Peace and Humanitarian Action

2013:

Simone de Beauvoir Prize for Women's Freedom, France

Nobel Peace Prize nominee

Sakharov Prize for Freedom of Thought – awarded by the European Parliament

Named one of *Time* magazine's "100 Most Influential People in the World"

International Children's Peace Prize

Vital Voices Global Leadership Awards, Global Trailblazer

OPEC Fund for International Development Award

Ambassador of Conscience Award from Amnesty International

Clinton Global Citizen Award

Harvard Foundation's Peter Gomes Humanitarian Award

Anna Politkovskaya Award – Reach All Women In War

Honorary Master of Arts degree from Edinburgh University

International Prize for Equality and Non-Discrimination, Mexico

United Nations Prize in the Field of Human Rights

2014:

Nobel Peace Prize, shared with India's Kailash Satyarthi

Skoll Global Treasure Award

Honorary Doctor of Civil Law, University of King's College, Halifax, Nova Scotia, Canada

Philadelphia Liberty Medal

Named one of "The 25 Most Influential Teens of 2014" by *Time* magazine

2015:

Grammy Award for Best Children's Album

Asteroid named in her honor

2017:

Youngest ever United Nations Messenger of Peace

Honorary doctorate from the University of Ottawa

Honorary Canadian citizenship

Ellis Island International Medal of Honor

TIMELINE

Malala Yousafzai born in Mingora in Swat Valley, Pakistan, to parents Ziauddin and Toor Pekai Yousafzai

1997

The Taliban extremist group takes over the Swat Valley

2007

Begins blogging for BBC Urdu at age 11 about life under the Taliban. Taliban orders girls' schools closed.

January 2009

May 2009

Family flees their home due to Taliban and army violence

July 2009

Family returns home and schools slowly reopen

Awarded Pakistan's National Peace Award for Youth, later named the Malala Award

November 2011

Shot in the head inside a school bus by the Taliban at age 15. After emergency surgery, flown to England for more treatment.

October 2012

Discharged from the hospital. Family remains in Birmingham, England.

January 2013

On her 16th birthday, addresses the United Nations in New York, her first public speech since the attack

July 2013

Malala Fund, started by Malala and her father. *I Am Malala* autobiography published.

October 2013

March 2013

Enters Edgbaston High School for girls in Birmingham, England

September 2013

Wins the 2013 International Children's Peace Prize from the Netherlands

Wins Nobel Peace Prize at age 17. Shares prize with Indian children's activist Kailash Satyarthi

October 2014

The documentary film *He Named Me Malala* debuts in 11 languages in 175 countries

October 2015

Addresses Canadian house of Parliament and named honorary citizen of Canada

August 2017

January 2019

New book *We Are Displaced: True Stories of Refugee Lives* set for publication

August 2017

Wins place at University of Oxford in England to study philosophy, politics, and economics. Starts there as a student.

April 2017

UN appoints her a UN Messenger of Peace to promote girls' education. At 19, she is youngest recipient ever.

March 2018

Malala Fund school for girls opens in her family's traditional village, Shangla, Pakistan. She and her family return to Pakistan and their hometown to visit for the first time since the shooting. She gives national speech on television.

April to September 2017

Takes "Girl Power Trip" to several nations to promote girls' education

July 2015

Opens school for displaced Syrian girls in Lebanon

GLOSSARY

Anne Frank: Dutch Jewish girl who wrote a diary in World War II; after her death the diary was published as an influential book, *The Diary of a Young Girl*.

asteroid: Small rocky bodies in space between planets.

cochlear implant: Device planted in the head near the ear to allow people to hear.

coma: State of unconsciousness caused by illness or injury.

conspiracy theorists: People who always see conspiracies instead of facts.

devout: Deeply religious.

Islamic: To do with the Muslim faith.

laureate: A person who has won an honor, also called a laurel, in the arts or sciences.

mullah: Educated Muslim in official post.

oratory: Eloquent public speaking.

Pashto: Language of the Pashtun people.

shalwar kameez: Pakistani women's dress.

social media trolls: People who try to cause trouble or mislead others on websites by posting angry or even false things.

Sunni: A branch of Islam.

symmetrical: The same on both sides.

Urdu: Official language of Pakistan.

zealot: Fanatical person.

FOR MORE INFORMATION

BOOKS

Doeden, Matt. *Malala Yousafzai: Shot by the Taliban, Still Fighting for Equal Education*. Minneapolis, MN: Lerner Publications, 2015.

Yousafzai, Malala, with Patricia McCormick. *I Am Malala: How One Girl Stood Up for Education and Changed the World*. New York, NY: Little, Brown, 2016.

Yousafzai, Malala, illustrated by Kerascoët. *Malala's Magic Pencil*. New York, NY: Little, Brown, 2017.

WEBSITES

www.malala.org
Malala Fund and Malala's blog

www.nobelprize.org/nobel_prizes/peace/
laureates/2014/yousafzai-lecture_en.html
Malala's Nobel Prize Lecture

INDEX